Original title:
Ocean's Gentle Call

Copyright © 2025 Creative Arts Management OÜ
All rights reserved.

Author: Maya Livingston
ISBN HARDBACK: 978-1-80581-639-3
ISBN PAPERBACK: 978-1-80581-166-4
ISBN EBOOK: 978-1-80581-639-3

The Sigh of Nautical Breezes

A seagull swoops with quite a flair,
It steals my lunch without a care.
I shout, "Hey bird, that's mine to munch!"
But he just laughs and takes a crunch.

The waves they giggle, splash and frollick,
While fish below form quite a collick.
They dart and dive, with silly grace,
Flipping their tails, a funny chase.

Traces of Portside Tranquility

A sailor's hat flies off his head,
A gust comes in, and I feel dread.
It spins around like it's on fire,
He chases it—quite the spectacle, sire!

The lighthouse blinks a cheeky eye,
While crabs and clams just wave goodbye.
They tease the boats with their silly games,
Pretending to win like they have great aims.

Resplendent Ripples

The sun dances on waves like a show,
While I trip on sand, oh what a woe!
I tumble right into a pile of goo,
The starfish giggle, "Oh look, it's you!"

A dolphin jumps, thinks he's a star,
With moves so slick, they travel afar.
But when he lands on a boat to pose,
He knocks the owner right on his nose!

Whispers in the Moonlight

The moon grins wide, watching a prank,
As a crab sneaks up to steal my drank.
He tries to tiptoe, but slips in the tide,
With a splash and a clatter, he takes a wild ride.

A couple of otters play tag and twist,
Splashing around, wave after mist.
They laugh and squeak, oh what a sight,
Under the stars, they frolic all night.

Waves of Remembrance

A seagull squawks, it steals my fries,
While fish below perform their dives.
I wave back at the splashing waves,
But all I get are soggy lays.

My bucket hat, a sight to see,
Blown off by gusts, it flies with glee.
The tide retreats, my laughter swells,
As all my snacks it stealthily quells.

Horizons Woven in Dreams

A sunburned crab, he scuttles by,
With tiny legs, oh my, oh my!
He looks like me when I try to dance,
With clumsy moves, not a single chance.

The sandcastles rise, then swiftly fall,
As waves come in, they heed the call.
My bucket's full of seashells bright,
I've done enough work, time for a bite!

The Soft Touch of Driftwood

I found a stick, but wait! What's this?
A treasure trove, oh pure bliss!
A flip-flop lost, it waves at me,
A liquid party, as fun as can be!

Driftwood whispers secrets old,
Tales of pirates and treasures bold.
I laugh aloud at their old plight,
Imagining my own sea-faring flight!

Cradled by the Marine Mist

With misty hair and salty kiss,
I chase my dreams, a breezy bliss.
The dolphins dance in playful glee,
I wave to them; they wink at me.

A rubber duck floats by my side,
In this grand sea, we take a ride.
I tell him jokes, he quacks so loud,
We're quite the duo, proud and loud!

Lanterns on the Water's Edge

The tide rolls in, what a greet!
Crabs scurry fast, tapping their feet.
A fish jumps high, right in my hat,
I swear it's plotting, what's up with that?

Seagulls giggle, they steal my fries,
I toss them crumbs, they flap and rise.
The sun winks down, a bright, cheeky glow,
Giggles echo where the waters flow.

Beneath the Sailor's Stars

A twinkling wink from stars above,
They know my secrets, a mischievous love.
Sails flap wildly, I hold on tight,
The wind's like a toddler in a kite fight.

A dolphin leaps, says hello with a splash,
I drop my drink, oh what a crash!
The night is alive, with waves and laughs,
Even the moon beams in goofy halves.

The Brush of Feathery Clouds

Clouds race by, a fluffy parade,
They take my thoughts, but they never stayed.
A seabreeze tickles, giving me cheer,
Zephyr's banter? Oh, let's steer clear!

A parrot jokes, "Polly wants to fly!"
I respond, "But only if I try!"
With laughter ringing from shore to shore,
The clouds just giggle, begging for more.

In the Lull of Your Wake

In the lull of waves, there's a rhythm strong,
Fish dance merrily, as if in a song.
The boat sways gently, rocks like a chair,
While clumsy sailors lose their flair!

A splash goes up, laughs echo around,
One slips and bounces, lands with a sound.
"Next time, guys, I'll stick to the dock!"
And yet in the mist, the fun never stops.

Rhythms of the Rolling Tide

A crab in a tux, takes a chance to dance,
Waving his claws, he thinks he has a chance.
The seagulls caw so loud, it's quite a mess,
As fish throw their bait, all in fancy dress.

The waves lick the shore, like hungry dogs,
While shells play poker with a band of frogs.
A dolphin flips pancakes, what a strange sight,
Splashing on seaglass under the moonlight.

Beneath the Glistening Foam

A starfish stuck in a skincare craze,
Requests a sea sponge for his facial phase.
Bubble-blowing octopuses roam the deep,
While jellyfish snooze in their frothy sleep.

Crab and shrimp argue, who's got a better shell,
While little minnows sing tunes, oh so swell.
The tide rolls in, and they chase it away,
So join in the fun, let's dance in the spray!

Memories of the Crimson Sunsets

The sun winks at dolphins who wave back in glee,
As surfers go tumbling, they spill their sweet tea.
With a splash of bright pink and a dash of bright gold,
The horizon looks like it's covered in mold.

Crabs throw a party, they're wearing loud hats,
While seaweed sways tall, like it's dancing with cats.
A clam tells a joke, it's a real stinker,
The sea turtles laugh, oh, what a great thinker!

Tranquil Hues of the Seascape

A fish with a mustache serves fishy cuisine,
While turtles tell tales of big waves they've seen.
Starry skies above and a moon made of cheese,
The currents do jiggles, just as they please.

Lobsters play sax, while crabs tap in time,
With squids doing flips, they're quite sublime.
The seafoam offers hugs, so soft and so bright,
As everyone laughs at this watery sight!

Shores of Endless Wonder

The tide comes in, a friend I know,
With laughter mixed in every flow.
It tickles toes, it splashes clothes,
As seagulls dance in silly pose.

Crabs in suits, they scuttle fast,
Pretending they're on a grandcast.
Sandcastles rise, then waves erase,
The builders chase with bright red face.

Beach balls bounce with joyful cheer,
While sunscreen's spread from ear to ear.
The sunburned clown in silly hat,
Just waves goodbye, then sits—how fat!

Down by the water, joys do swell,
Where laughter echoes, oh so well.
Each splash a giggle, wild and free,
Life's funny dance in harmony.

The Calm Between the Tempests

Between the storms, we pause and play,
With silly jokes to save the day.
The fish they laugh in bubbles bright,
As sailors sing through day and night.

A pirate's parrot takes a dive,
To steal a snack, just to survive.
With rainclouds looming in the back,
He squawks out jokes, a real wisecrack.

We ride the waves, both far and near,
While dolphins dance, we hold our beer.
The storm may come, the sails may rip,
But we're all smiles on this wild trip.

Laughter rings across the bay,
As seabirds join the grand ballet.
The calm before, it makes us laugh,
As we share tales, both bold and daft.

Notes from the Coral Reefs

In coral halls, where colors blend,
Fish tell tales, their fins extend.
A bass with shades, so posh and neat,
Claims he found the world's best beat.

Anemones sway, they simply glide,
While clownfish giggle, side by side.
A turtle sings a lovely tune,
Swaying gently 'neath the moon.

With jellyfish in disco lights,
They twirl and swirl on dreamy nights.
A shrimp in boots with fancy flair,
Drops the beat with style to spare.

These notes from depths where laughter blooms,
Turn every tide into bright cartoons.
Coral laughter, wild and bright,
Resounds beneath the moon's soft light.

Wanderlust in the Seascape

With salty breeze and sunlit trails,
We chase the dreams where laughter sails.
Seashells whisper tales from far,
While gulls perform their circus star.

A fish in shades of neon glow,
Tells me which way to go.
Crab chases after floating fries,
While I just giggle through the skies.

The ship's crew sings their shanty song,
As deckside antics march along.
A mermaid joins, she's quite a tease,
As dolphins frolic with great ease.

Wanderlust calls with jovial cheer,
To dance with waves, year after year.
In every splash and every breeze,
Laughter reigns, and we're at ease.

Beneath the Shimmering Surface

Bubbles dance and twirl around,
As fish wear hats, they swim astound.
A crab does the cha-cha, full of cheer,
While seaweed sways to music near.

A clam told a joke that made me grin,
He said, 'Life's a beach, so let's dive in!'
Turtles laugh as they float on by,
While dolphins plot a sky-high pie.

Starfish juggling shells on the sand,
With sand dollars who critique the band.
An octopus performs sleight of hand,
While cheering up the crabby land.

With bubbles and giggles, the waves call,
Under the sun, we're having a ball.
Each splash a laugh, each shore a game,
In this watery world, we're never the same.

Driftwood Dreams

A piece of driftwood, with quite the tale,
Claimed he'd been a ship, then turned to snail.
Seagulls cackled, oh what a sight,
While crabs debated who'd take the flight.

A starfish yawned, said, 'I'll pass, my friend,
For rolling in these tides is the latest trend.'
With barnacles joining in on the fun,
They threw a beach party under the sun.

The jellyfish twirled with style so grand,
While clams served snacks made of fine sand.
A sea cucumber whispered, "What's the scoop?"
And they all joined in a giant flip-flop loop.

As shells collected tales of the day,
Driftwood dreams drifted the night away.
With laughter and splashes, they danced under stars,
In this funny realm, no one needs cars.

Embracing Gentle Waters

The water's hug is soft and warm,
Where fish wear pajamas, oh what a charm!
They swim in circles, playing tag,
While sea cucumbers give a brag.

Whales try to sing, but sounds turn squeaks,
Seahorses giggle, and here it peaks!
A dance of bubbles floats by our toes,
As the tide winds down and laughter grows.

Anemones throw a foam-filled bash,
Decorating their homes with colorful trash.
With each wave, a joke drifts ashore,
"Why don't fish play piano?" — "They can't find the score!"

With flippers and fins, friends gather close,
In waters that shine more than a toast.
Together they splash, together they play,
In this funny sea, life's a grand ballet.

A Symphony of Pebbles

Pebbles roll to the rhythm of the tide,
Wiggling together, they take a ride.
A rock grumbled, 'Why am I so round?'
While others laughed, 'You've got the sound!'

A pebble orchestra begins to play,
With shells as speakers leading the way.
Sand dollars tap dance on the shore,
While fish applaud, begging for more!

A jellyfish pops up, joins the fun,
Swaying and gliding like a quirky bun.
Dancing to rhythms that shift with the foam,
Together they sing, "We're never alone!"

As the sun sets down, and stars take their place,
Pebbles still jive, though they're slowing the pace.
In this silly show, laughter rings true,
With pebbles and shells, life's never askew.

The Rhythm of the Surf

The waves dance and wiggle with glee,
Singing a tune with a splashy decree.
Seagulls on hover, joking with style,
Workin' their charm, all while in a pile.

Beach balls are bouncing, oh what a sight,
Running from kids who are quick with delight.
Sandcastles groan under each tiny foot,
"Oh please spare me!" they seem to hoot.

Tranquility in Blue

Beneath the blue, there's a joke or two,
Starfish are giggling and pranking the crew.
Crabs in their shells, they scurry with grace,
Trying to win the best race on the base.

Turtles in shades, looking oh-so-cool,
Swimmin' in circles, they're breaking the rule.
"Just keep swimming," they cheer with a chuckle,
While humans just sit, in the sun, they struggle.

Secrets of the Distant Shore

Whispers of sand fill the salty air,
Fish tell tall tales, oh, they'll never share!
Mighty waves crash, but it's just in jest,
They'll tickle your toes, never let you rest.

Driftwood lounges, sunbathing in style,
"Hey there, come join me!" it says with a smile.
Seashells conspire, plotting their plots,
Hiding the treasures but laughing a lot.

The Tide's Soft Invitation

The tide called me over, I answered with glee,
But tripped on a wave, it was laughing at me!
Unleashed waves quip, "Come play if you dare!"
Gently they splash, while I flounder and stare.

The sun flashed a grin, shining down unashamed,
And seaweed joined in, though it felt quite maimed.
Together we jive, a silly parade,
Nature's grand jest, that will never fade.

Driftwood Dreams in the Dusk

A stick floats by, with dreams to share,
Gossiping shells toss back their hair.
Jellyfish dance in ridiculous style,
While crabs do their best to walk a mile.

Seagulls squawk in a messy chorus,
They dive for fries, oh what a fuss!
A buoy waves hello, quite a charmer,
Who knew it had such gossip and glamour?

In the twilight, laughter and splashes,
Sandcastles rise but fall in crashes.
A clam in the sand throws a beach ball high,
While a wandering whale just passes by.

The dusk is a stage, with antics galore,
Every wave giggles, every tide roars.
With driftwood dreams painting skies aglow,
Even the tide knows how to put on a show.

Where the Sand Meets Serenity

At the shore, my flip-flops flew,
Chasing crabs—they giggled too!
A game of tag, so completely absurd,
Who knew crustaceans could be so stirred?

Seashells argue over who's the best,
One claims it's the one with a tiny nest.
Sunbathers snicker, umbrellas in three,
While a rogue wave steals your sun tea.

With sand in sandwiches, and waves in hair,
Life's little mishaps just add to the flair.
Kites in the sky, tugged by the breeze,
Try to escape, like wild runaway keys!

So here at the shore, laughter's the rule,
Finding joy in the weird and the cool.
For where the grains meet the soft, sweet foam,
Even the silly finds a place called home.

Reflections on Aqua Mirrors

The sea reflects, in fits of cheer,
Fish wear glasses and wiggle near.
A dolphin tries to photobomb,
While fishes giggle in perfect calm.

Sunbathers are frying, but oh what a sight,
With SPF battles, who'll last the night?
A buoy bragged, it can float all day,
But tipsy crabs have something to say.

In the shallows, laughter bubbles bright,
A starfish drops its shades, oh what a fright!
With seaweed hair, they twirl with grace,
While a whale tells tales in a deep-water space.

The horizon giggles, bringing forth day,
While mermaids practice their dolphin ballet.
In reflections of life, with a comedic twist,
The water's calm, but it's laughter we miss.

Cherished Days by the Seaside

We built a castle, so proud and tall,
Then watched it dwindle with one little squall.
A toddler's scoop, and whoops, there it goes,
The tide laughed harder than anyone knows.

With ice cream drips all over the place,
Seagulls steal bites with their sneaky grace.
A splash fight breaks out—oh what fun!
Paddles and giggles under the sun.

Beach towels dance like they're in a show,
As sunscreen battles the heat's fiery glow.
With flop and roll, we stumble and sway,
Each cherished moment, a whimsical play.

At day's end, we wave our goodbyes,
With sandy toes and sun-kissed skies.
For in these precious seaside hours,
We found laughter in nature's flowers.

Lullabies from Deep Waters

The fish sing songs in their scales,
While jellyfish float on jelly trails.
A crab in pajamas does a little jig,
As seaweed sways like a dancing pig.

The starfish clap with five-pointed hands,
While seahorses wave like marching bands.
An octopus plays on a violin,
And the clownfish laugh till the day begins.

A whale rides waves like a bumpy bus,
And dolphins giggle, causing a fuss.
The sea turtles waddle, oh what a sight,
With shells shining brightly under the moonlight.

So come take a dip in this watery land,
Where every creature has a funny hand.
With laughter and bubbles, we'll splash away,
In the giggle-filled waters of play-filled bay.

Currents of Serenity

The waves roll in, a tickle and tease,
A sea snail sneezes with the greatest of ease.
Crabs wear hats made from seashells round,
In this funny place where laughter is found.

Starfish float by on their lazy spree,
Complaining about sea life, oh woe is he!
A whale shares jokes about living the deep,
While the fish all chuckle and giggle in sleep.

A sandy beach party with snacks made of sand,
Where mermaids serve drinks with a handstand.
The tide comes in with a swish and a swoosh,
Inviting the tidepools to join in the push.

So grab a floatie, come join the cheer,
In currents of laughter, there's nothing to fear.
Dive headfirst into the splashy delight,
Where each wave whispers a joke, oh so bright!

Dance of the Driftwood

Driftwood sways with a groovy beat,
As barnacles join with their funky feet.
A seagull croons from atop a pole,
While a sea urchin rolls with its spiky soul.

The seashells click in a rhythmic way,
As crabs get busy dancing the day.
Underwater parties that shake and roll,
As fish in tuxedos take on their role.

The current spins wild in a whirl of fun,
With a conch shell DJ, the party's begun.
The eel's breakdancing, oh what a sight,
As the waves get groovy under the moonlight.

So come to the shore, bring laughter and cheer,
In this driftwood dance, there's nothing to fear.
Join the odd critters as they twist and twirl,
In the funny, fishy, fabulous world!

Horizon's Embrace

The sunset chuckles, painting the sky,
As clouds turn pink, oh me, oh my!
Seagulls swoop with a laugh in the air,
While waves tickle toes without any care.

A fisherman's hat floats past with glee,
Chasing a fish on a surfboard spree.
The sandcastles giggle as tides come to knock,
As starfish wear crowns made from a rock.

The horizon says jokes that the sun can't tell,
While mermaids splash in a sparkling well.
An otter pretends it's a tin can boat,
While turtles make tea on a driftwood coat.

So let's frolic and laugh as the day winds down,
In this whimsical place, wear smiles, not frowns.
With every splash and each roar of the surf,
Horizon's embrace gives comedic rebirth!

Murmurs of the Maritime Mist

A fish wore a hat, what a sight,
Swim lessons for crabs, all in delight.
They danced on the waves, quite the show,
Teasing a dolphin with a big belly blow.

Seagulls were laughing, what a flock,
Trying to steal a sandwich from a rock.
A crab said, 'Be nice, let's share this treat,'
But the seagulls just squawked, 'You can't be beat!'

Starfish were lounging, catching sun,
Building a castle, having some fun.
A clam yelled out, 'Hey, look at me!'
But the sand said, 'You're stuck, poor old sea!'

They all laughed together, what a crew,
As temps dropped low, the sky turned blue.
When waves rolled in, they'd hitch a ride,
With fish as their mates, they'd splash and glide.

Secrets of the Deep Blue

Down below, where the funny fish play,
A squid starts a conga, in quite the way.
Anglerfish winked with a glow so bright,
While turtles danced in a dazzling light.

Octopus plans for a costume spree,
Puffs up in bubbles, just wait and see!
The lobsters giggle, in their fancy shells,
Spinning some tales like oceanic bells.

Seahorses giggle in a twirling craze,
Trying to play tag in a coral maze.
But their tails got tangled, what a sight,
Rolling with laughter, oh what pure delight!

A treasure chest opened, oh what a find!
Rubies and bubbles, all intertwined.
The fish turned to dance, one final swirl,
As seaweed joined in, twirling and twirl!

Graceful Embrace of the Surf

On sandy shores, a wave said, 'Hi!'
Check out my flip—oh, don't be shy!
Surfboards bob like a wobbly cake,
While seagulls swoop in for a quick break.

A crab in shades thought he was cool,
Claiming the tide was his favorite pool.
Seashells giggled as they rolled on by,
'You're a star, little crab, give it a try!'

The sandcastles boast, 'We won't fall down!'
But a rogue wave had a different crown.
Pushed by the tide, they laughed in vain,
Temporary kings, then gone again!

A clam with a grin said, 'What's the fuss?'
All we need is some laughter and trust.
With fish and a splash, they twirled with glee,
Making beaches a place of pure jubilee.

Shores of Dreams and Dusk

As stars peek out, the waves tickle sand,
Crabs play charades, at the moon's command.
A jellyfish boogies, oh what a sight,
With the tide pulling in, he twirls left and right.

Seagulls serenade with a comical tune,
Hoping for snacks that have come too soon.
They shouted, 'Hey fish, don't be a fool!'
But the fish just blew bubbles, looking so cool.

The sand whispered secrets to the shells,
Of grand fishy trips and their quirky tales.
Each wave that rolled carried laughter's sound,
As dreams on the shore spun round and round.

With the dusk painting skies, colors profound,
Crabs shared their stories, and joy did abound.
On those shores of dreams, with giggles and cheer,
Life dances on water, so precious and dear.

Reflections on Silken Waters

In the mirror of the sea, I stand,
Watching fish dance like a band.
They wiggle and jiggle, what a sight,
Trying to catch a wave of light.

Seagulls squawk, they steal my fries,
With beady eyes, oh what a surprise!
They swoop and loop, a cheeky crew,
While I sip my soda, what can I do?

The tide rolls in, it tickles my toes,
A splash of water, quick as it goes.
I laugh and shout, 'You can't get me!'
But the wave just giggles, 'Wait and see!'

Floating along like a cork in a whirl,
Dreaming of mermaids with hair in a twirl.

Where the Sky Meets the Sea

Up above, the clouds play tricks,
Casting shadows, doing flips.
Down below, the crabs are quick,
Dancing sideways, oh what a kick!

The sun plays peek-a-boo all day,
While dolphins seem to shout, "Hooray!"
I wave back, feeling quite bold,
It's like a party, all gold in gold.

A boat sails by, it's filled with cheer,
Sailing on laughter, not a fear.
I toss a line to catch a breeze,
But just a fish says, "Mind your peas!"

Where the sky kisses the sea's embrace,
The waves go splashing like a playful race.

A Voyage Through Serenity

Set my sail for a trip so grand,
Off to a place with soft, warm sand.
The captain calls, "All aboard!"
But I'm busy with my snack hoard.

Seashells giggle as I wander near,
"I'd trade you for chips!" they seem to sneer.
Starfish shrug, "We're all in this mess,"
While crabs just dance in their shell dress.

I spotted a whale, he's singing a tune,
Underneath the big bright moon.
He says, "Join me for a splashy song!"
I replied, "Happy to, let's get along!"

Riding the waves, we leap and glide,
Through all the fun, I cannot hide.

Melodies of the Briny Deep

Bubbles rise like laughter loud,
Underwater jokes with the fishy crowd.
Octopuses juggle, seaweed flails,
While I'm here with my snack-filled pails.

Nautical tunes drift soft and slow,
As turtles groove and put on a show.
Bending back for a clam ballet,
An unexpected twist to greet the day.

With each wave, the frolics grow,
As jellyfish bob and steal the show.
"Dance with us," they seem to plea,
I let out a chuckle, "Just wait, you'll see!"

Melodies linger in salty air,
I join the fun without a care.

A Heartbeat of the Moonlit Sea

The waves dance like a funny clown,
With splashes that go up and down.
The moon winks with a silver smile,
As fish giggle and swim in style.

Sand crabs wearing tiny hats,
Are marching in their little spats.
With each wave they're swept around,
What a jolly little sound!

Starfish whisper silly jokes,
While seagulls share their bread and hoax.
Mermaids laugh, they're having fun,
In their world, there's never done.

The tide brings shenanigans galore,
With giggles echoing to the shore.
Splashing water, wild and carefree,
Life's a comedy beneath the sea.

The Call of Aquatic Dreams

In dreams I float on a rubber duck,
With fish who give me luck.
They wear glasses and read the news,
Trading gossip and silly views.

Octopuses painting with flair,
Coloring corals, beyond compare.
Dolphins joke and jump on cue,
Outfitting themselves in shades of blue.

A pirate parrot squawks with glee,
"Who's up for treasure? Just follow me!"
But all he finds are slippery slides,
Where laughter splashes and fun abides.

From depths to shallows, it's quite a scene,
Where seaweed sways in a seaweed sheen.
In this world of whimsy and cheer,
Every wave brings a new kind of year.

Embracing the Salty Air

The sea breeze tickles my face,
As seagulls dance and find their place.
A crab in shades walks by with style,
Waving hello with a goofy smile.

The salty air is full of cheer,
As mermaids play their ukuleles near.
With each strum a bubble pops,
And laughter rises as the music stops.

Frisky fishes in a conga line,
Twisting and turning, feeling fine.
They stop to wink and steal a glance,
At a curious crab doing a dance.

Far away, a whale gives a blow,
Spraying water in a marvelous show.
Life here is a giggling spree,
With every breath, we're wild and free.

Interlude with the Sea Foam

Sea foam frolics like a playful pup,
Tickling toes as it bubbles up.
Waves sing songs of joy and delight,
While surfers attempt their highest flight.

With jellyfish dressed for a masquerade,
Each one gleams with a sparkly shade.
They twirl and spin, in jelly-like grace,
Making sure they steal the show's space.

A starfish on the shore starts to strut,
Shouting, "Look at me, I'm really cut!"
But the tide washes it back with a laugh,
A slippery, giggling photograph.

So here's to the chuckles and playful waves,
The joy of the sea, where laughter saves.
With each frothy splash, we forget our woes,
In this silly, salty world that glows.

Embracing the Celestial Sea

Sandy toes and crabs that dance,
Seagulls giggling, taking their chance.
The waves whisper jokes, oh, so sly,
While starfish laugh as they flip by.

A fish in a tux, oh what a sight,
Waves in the sun, oh what a delight.
The crab's got moves that make you cheer,
As they shimmy and shake with no hint of fear.

Beach balls bounce and sunscreen flies,
The tide rolls in with silly surprise.
Flip-flops toss and umbrellas spin,
As laughter erupts from where we've been.

So come, take a dip in this mirthful sea,
Where every wave holds a giggle, you see!
Expect the unexpected, let your heart sway,
In this playful world, we'll splash all day.

Tidepooling in Twilight

With the stars peeking over the bay,
We gawk at creatures that giggle and sway.
A sea cucumber making a fuss,
While crabs argue over a shiny bus.

The octopus prances, a real show-off,
Trying to steal the spotlight, a real goof-off.
Where jellyfish float with such funny grace,
While clumsy starfish fall flat on their face.

Tide pools bubble, a comedic affair,
As anemones sway like they just don't care.
A mollusk whispered, "Hey, look at me!"
In this twilight waltz with salty glee.

As the sun dips low, and laughter surrounds,
We chase the waves, making silly sounds.
With each splash and giggle, our joy ignites,
In a world full of wonder on starry nights.

The Gentle Lure of the Horizon

A rubber duck sails on this bluest sea,
Winking at fish as they swim carefree.
The gulls are rehearsing their stand-up act,
While sea urchins ponder how to react.

We build castles where laughs run wild,
As crabs critique the work of a child.
"More towers!" they say, "Taller and grand!"
The little ones giggle, giving a hand.

The sun flips around in a playful jest,
As bright pink seashells join the fest.
Each wave a tickle, each splash so bold,
Creatures chuckling, their stories retold.

"Float like a jelly!" one seagull shouts,
While a dolphin whistles, dispelling doubts.
In the glow of the sunset, we dance and twirl,
Chasing the horizon, laughter unfurled.

In the Company of Silent Waves

Whispers of water, a soft little hum,
As clams tell tales while crabs go `dumb`!
A fish pretends it's a Hollywood star,
Waving at viewers from afar.

The waves giggle and roll like a kid,
As sea turtles dance, trying to skib.
Where seaweed sways like an awkward teen,
And barnacles gossip of places they've been.

An otter floats, polishing a shell,
Singing the blues, oh, can you tell?
While sea stars laugh at the silly scene,
Making the ocean feel like a dream.

So come, join the fun in this watery space,
Where humor and tides have a jovial pace.
Each wave a giggle, each splash a cheer,
With every moment, happiness near!

The Gentle Breath of the Tide

The waves roll in with a playful sway,
Knocking over sandcastles made that day.
A crab scurries by, a sideways dance,
Who knew crustaceans had such a chance?

Seagulls squawk with a cheeky glee,
Stealing fries as they hide in a tree.
The sun plays peek-a-boo, hides then appears,
While beach balls bounce, igniting our cheers.

A dolphin jumps, a mischievous sight,
Winking at us, as he takes flight.
With each clap of the wave, laughter's the tune,
An underwater party starts too soon!

So grab your floaties, we'll paddle away,
Trading childhood for flippers and play.
As the tide calls out, with a wink and a smile,
We know we'll stay for just a short while.

Footprints on the Sandy Shore

With feet in the sand, squishing away,
You'd think I'd learn, oh but not today!
My flip-flop flops, my balance a joke,
As I tumble ahead, like a clumsy folk.

A line of footprints, oddly arranged,
Look like a dance that's perfectly strange.
Each step I take, the tide says hi,
Swishing my shoes, oh my, oh my!

In the distance, a child starts to scream,
A seagull just swiped his ice cream!
I laugh till I ache, what a comical scene,
The taste of salty air, and the sweet of the cream.

As I stroll along this sandy spree,
I trip over shells, it's just meant to be.
With giggles amid the waves that roar,
These footprints tell tales, and oh, so much more!

Celestial Echoes of the Deep

Beneath the waves where the bubbles rise,
A fish flops by, with surprise in his eyes.
He twirls in circles, putting on a show,
As I crack up at Submarine Joe.

The starfish lounge, so chill and relaxed,
While clams click their shells, puzzled and taxed.
"What's all the fuss?" their chatter does say,
"Oh look, here comes another beachgoer's stray!"

An octopus dances, with arms in a twist,
Who knew the ocean could be such a tryst?
Echoes of laughter bounce off the coral,
As fish throw a party that's borderline floral!

So here in the deep, where it's lively and bright,
We giggle with glee at the wriggly sight.
With celestial wonders, laughter will seep,
In the bubbly of giggles, so joyful, so deep!

Twilight Serenades of the Coast

As the sun dips low, the sky turns to gold,
Seagulls are belting songs, never too old.
With a twirl of their wings, they emit quite the squawk,
While beachgoers laugh and start dancing the jock.

The sand is a canvas, we scatter our dreams,
While shadows of friends play out in moonbeams.
A raccoon appears, thinking it's a buffet,
He snatches a sandwich, then nibbles away!

The tide crests and splashes, a splash zone for all,
As I dodge the water, but hear my name call.
Oh wait, there's my friend, he trips on a log,
Here comes the laughter, out pops the fog!

So we sip on our drinks, as the stars start to glow,
On this quirky coastline, laughter's the flow.
With twilight's embrace and waves that refuse,
The serenade continues, we'll never lose!

Dawn's Embrace on Salted Shores

The sun peeks in, a golden grin,
Seagulls squawk, let the day begin.
Tans turn to lobster in midday sun,
While crabs dance sideways, oh what fun!

Beach balls fly, like fish in the air,
Ice cream drips, a sticky affair.
Kids laugh loud, as waves chase their toes,
Shells hide secrets that nobody knows.

A dog digs deep, for treasures below,
But finds just sand, and a sharp toe.
Mom's sun hat flies, in a sudden breeze,
The chase is on, as she squeals with ease!

The tide rolls in, with a playful kiss,
Each splash and giggle is pure bliss.
Dawn's embrace wraps us in delight,
As we dance and leap until the night.

The Treasure of Aquatic Whispers

Bubbles rise, like secrets shared,
Mermaids gossip, though none were cared.
Fish flip-flop, in synchronized style,
Waves giggle softly, with salty guile.

An octopus waves, with too many hands,
While jellyfish bob like free-floating bands.
Crabby chefs serve up seaweed stew,
While turtles ponder, 'What's for me and you?'

A treasure chest holds glittering dreams,
But it's just full of mismatched seams.
Dolphins joke with a splash and a spin,
"Who's cooler, us or that fish with a fin?"

With each corkscrew dive, hilarity reigns,
As sea creatures play, shunning the chains.
The warmth of tides calls out to play,
In this underwater cabaret!

Where Waves Meet the Sky

Where sea and sky join in a dance,
Waves twirl and leap, full of chance.
Clouds drift low, like puffy sheep,
While surfers ride, not a single peep.

At sunset's glow, colors collide,
To paint the horizon, in swell and tide.
But wait, what's that? A dolphin's jest,
"He's riding high, bet I can rest!"

Sandcastles crumble, their royalty gone,
As children laugh, and dusk lingers on.
The wind whispers tales of days long past,
Of silly seagulls, oh what a blast!

In this place, joy mingles with glee,
Nature's canvas, wild and free.
Where antics reign and spirits soar,
At the edge of the waves, forevermore!

Composing with the Current

A symphony swells in the salty air,
As fish ensemble, without a care.
Conducted by currents, in a playful phase,
With crabs snapping rhythm, in quirky ways.

Seashells ring like castanets bright,
While starfish keep beat, with all their might.
The tide rolls out, but don't sound the alarm,
It's just pulling strings, orchestrating charm!

Oh! Listen close, to the jellyfish hum,
As the starry night tumbles into the fun.
Tides whisper softly, secrets to all,
While the moonlight dances, in cosmic thrall.

With every wave, laughter takes flight,
In this watery world, everything's right.
Composing together, in harmony's call,
Adventures await, and we'll have a ball!

Lanterns of the Evening Tide.

The fish wear hats and dance at night,
They grope for snacks, what a silly sight!
Jellyfish swing by making a fuss,
While octopuses cheer, riding a bus.

Crabs wear shoes that are way too big,
Tap-dancing away, they spin and jig!
Seaweed sways, it's the latest craze,
While snails race shells, putting on displays.

Starfish gossip about the best tide,
Whispering secrets, they can't decide!
Seahorses laugh, they've got jokes to share,
Puffers puff up with a comical flare.

Under the moon, the rhythm's alive,
Barnacles join in, they groove and jive!
With every splash, there's boundless cheer,
In this underwater party, we all are here.

Whispers of the Tides

A crab in a tux bids the waves goodnight,
While clam shells chatter, such a curious sight!
The dolphins giggle in synchronized fun,
As they leap through the air, oh what a run!

A squid with a pen scribbles tales from the deep,
His ink becomes poetry, making waves leap!
Starry fish twirl in a ballet so grand,
While shrimp hold a banquet with snacks made of sand.

Seagulls converse with a side of a sigh,
Over snacks dropped by the boats sailing by.
"Who's stealing my chips?" cries a flustered fish,
While mermaids just laugh and munch their own dish.

With bubbles and giggles, the sea crew aligns,
For laughter and splashes by moonlight, it shines.
Tales spun by sea, quite absurd yet sublime,
Their echoes reflect through the tides of time.

Beneath the Waves' Embrace

Down where the sea cucumbers do the twirl,
And clownfish wear makeup, giving a whirl!
Seahorses strut in adorable rows,
While conch shells gossip; do you hear how it goes?

Turtles strike poses, like models on sand,
With swagger and smiles, they look quite grand!
Anemones blush with the tickles they bring,
As they play with the fish in a soft underwater fling.

A walrus trips over a curious clam,
And all the young otters just giggle and jam.
With bubbles as balloons, they soar and they dive,
While sea stars applaud at the fun that's alive.

Each splash brings a chuckle, a giggle, a cheer,
For down in the deep, there's no room for fear!
The ridges of coral are delighted to see,
All the clownish antics below the blue sea!

Echoes of the Sea Breeze

The seagulls conspire, what mischief to find,
Stealing hot fries, oh, they're feeling so kind!
With a swoop and a glide, they cackle with glee,
As sardines all huddle, planning to flee.

A fish with a mustache tells jokes in the gale,
While sea urchins chuckle, they roll and they flail!
With bubbles like giggles that burst in the air,
The ocean's a stage, no worries or care.

Whales draft letters with a splash and a song,
Flowing through currents, where do they belong?
On waves made of laughter, they swim with finesse,
Cartwheeling waves in a buoyant dress.

So raise up a seashell and call out with cheer,
Join in the fun that the tides bring near!
Every splash is a story, in water's embrace,
Creating a rhythm, our own special place.

The Lullaby of the Deep

The fish sing songs of silly cheer,
While crabs do a jig, oh dear, oh dear!
Starfish watching, trying to clap,
But they just fall over, what a mishap!

A mermaid sneezes, bubbles fly,
A dolphin giggles, soaring high.
Seaweed sways to a funky beat,
As turtles groove with flippers, neat!

Squid ink portraits on ocean walls,
Clownfish cracking jokes, what a ball!
Sea urchins join, all sharp and round,
Creating a stage on the ocean ground!

So laugh along with the waves at play,
Undersea antics brighten the day.
Join the dance with every splash,
For in this world, there's always a clash!

Serenade of the Saltwater

The crab's a dancer, prancing 'round,
While a sea cucumber makes not a sound.
A shark tries to tell a fishy tale,
But forgets his punchline, begins to wail!

An octopus paints with all its arms,
Each stroke a giggle, capturing charms.
Jellyfish float with glittery grace,
While seagulls squawk, just making a face!

Sandcastles tumble, the tide says hi,
While clam shells whisper, "Why even try?"
The seafoam giggles, a bubbly mess,
As tides keep rolling, causing distress!

In salty depths where laughter's free,
The ocean knows how to get silly.
So dive right in, don't be too weird,
For every splash means fun is near!

Murmurs from the Abyss

Deep beneath where the squids all dwell,
An old pufferfish starts to tell
Of treasure maps and lost pirate dreams,
But ended up missing his popcorn seams!

The anglerfish flashes a light too bright,
Saying, "Be cautious, don't start a fight!"
But a sardine rolls in, a wiggle and jig,
And suddenly the abyss feels like a gig!

Crustaceans argue over a shiny shell,
While a whale whispers, "All is well!"
A stingray swoops, making quite a flair,
As laughter echoes through depths so rare!

So listen closely, hear the fun roar,
As the sea reveals its whimsical lore.
In the dark where shadows creep,
Lighthearted jests from the ocean deep!

A Dance with the Horizon

The sun dips low, waves begin to sway,
While barnacles gossip about their day.
Seagulls spin in a comical flight,
Chasing their shadows, what a silly sight!

Crabs in a row march with glee,
Waving their claws for all to see.
Starfish playing leapfrog on the sand,
What a curious, joyous band!

The wind hums tunes, rustling the kelp,
As fish play tag, not thinking of help.
The horizon giggles, painted with light,
Inviting all creatures to join the night!

So let's waltz together, hand in fin,
With every movement, let the fun begin.
Under moonlit skies, a shimmer of joy,
As nature's laughter, no one can destroy!

Reverie in Salt-Kissed Air

A seagull stole my sandwich, you see,
While I chased it, laughing, carefree.
The waves giggled, splashed at my toes,
As I tripped over seaweed like a clumsy pros.

The sun took a break behind puffy clouds,
A crowd of beachgoers cheered so loud.
With sunscreen smeared on my nose and chin,
I danced with the tides, let the fun begin!

My flip-flops flopped, my hat flew away,
Chasing the breeze, I joined the fray.
An octopus waved, no inkling of care,
As I awkwardly shouted, "Hey! Don't you dare!"

Caught in the rhythm, I made quite a splash,
A crab rolled his eyes, likely thought I was brash.
With laughter in waves, I gallivanted high,
In a saltwater world, where joy waves goodbye!

Solace Beneath the Coral

A starfish tried to wear my flip-flop shoe,
But it stumbled a bit, then said, "What's new?"
We giggled together in the sun's warm glow,
As fish played tag, putting on quite the show.

The turtle had jokes, so wise and so slow,
He shared underwater secrets that only we know.
"Why did the fish wear a bowtie today?"
"To look like a catch, or so they say!"

Sandcastles crumbled with each little wave,
While crabs threw a party, all bold and brave.
I joined the parade, feeling light as a plume,
As they danced on the shore, bringing laughter and bloom.

Underwater friends had mermaid hairdos,
With shells for crown jewels, oh what a muse!
Each splash was a giggle, each wave was a tease,
In the realm of the coral, nothing was a breeze!

Enchanted Waterscape

Seashells whispered riddles, a playful affair,
While dolphins leaped high with a flick of their flair.
"Why did the clam never share its deep pearl?"
"Because it was shy, in its own little whirl!"

A jellyfish jiggled, oh what a sight,
With a disco ball glow that lit up the night.
"Join me!" it beckoned, "Let's twirl and just sway,
Forget all our worries, and dance with the spray!"

With each playful splash, a new giggle arose,
As sea turtles tangoed, striking lyrical pose.
"Who brought the snacks?" yelled a fish dressed in gold,
"Let's feast on seaweed, the best to behold!"

The tide rolled its laughter, a soft, frothy roar,
While I joined the fish chorus, yelling encore!
The seagulls cawed, taking part in the jest,
In this enchanted waterscape, life is a fest!

The Melody of Distant Horizons

The sun sang a tune as it dipped in the bay,
While crabs held a concert, all ready to play.
With shells as their instruments, they bopped with a grin,
As the ocean clapped back, inviting the din.

A whale, quite the diva, performed with a splash,
Harmonizing with gulls in a melodic mash.
"Why are mermaids late?" asked a clam with a laugh,
"Because they get caught up in seashell craft!"

The stars twinkled brightly in the evening sky,
While sandpipers danced, giving the breeze a try.
"Did you hear the one about the sand dune's weight?"
"It said, 'I'm getting bigger—just waiting on fate!'"

With joy in each ripple, the horizon turned gold,
As laughter cascaded, a truth to behold.
In this world of whimsy, where silliness reigns,
The melody of life glides over the plains!

The Softest Current

A fish in a tux, quite out of place,
Dances on waves, with a silly face.
The jellyfish giggles, floats like a crown,
A party in blue, where no one frowns.

Seagulls throw shade with their dramatic flair,
Screaming for fries, without a care.
The crab brings the snacks, a shellfish delight,
Every wave brings laughter, from morning to night.

Sandcastles topple with giggles so loud,
As kids chase the tide, feeling quite proud.
A beach ball flies, hits a poor sunbather,
Who jumps with surprise, what a silly tater!

So come take a dip, let your worries float,
Join in the fun on this surfboard boat.
With tickling waves and a wink from the sun,
Life by the sea is a laugh-filled run.

Intertwined with Seafoam

A crab wears a hat, quite the big deal,
While fish do the cha-cha, oh what a reel!
With shells as their instruments, they make quite a sound,

Seafoam confetti, swirling all around.

The octopus juggles, so clumsy yet fierce,
He trips on a starfish — oh dear, it's a pierce!
Seashells are clapping, the dolphins all cheer,
As sea cucumbers groan, 'Must we stay here?'

Seagulls trade jokes, with a caw and a cackle,
One drops a sandwich, oh what a debacle!
With laughter and splashes, the tide rolls on through,
In this underwater circus, there's always a view.

So gather your friends, let the fun take a dive,
Where the waves are alive, and sea critters thrive.
As we twirl with the tide in a whimsically swirl,
Let's ride this wild wave, give the sea a whirl!

Amidst Floating Stars

Bubbles like balloons, float up to the sky,
A seal's on a surfboard, oh my, oh my!
The starfish, a dancer, twirls in the foam,
While crabs shoot the breeze, feeling quite at home.

The mermaids all giggle, tossing shells for a game,
Each wave a new chance, nothing is the same.
With laughter and splashes, the water does sing,
As the sun takes a bow, in a dazzling fling.

The fish start a band, with fins made of sound,
A sea cow conducts, waving arms all around.
In this watery concert, no one feels shy,
Just join in the fun, give a flip and a sigh.

So drift with the tide, let your worries all fade,
Amidst floating stars, where magic is made.
For the sea holds a secret, a whimsical call,
That tickles the soul, let's dance through it all!

When the Waters Sing

The wave crashes down, with a comedic splash,
A dolphin named Dave makes a daring dash.
While gulls squawk a tune, like a clumsy ballet,
It's a musical ocean, come join in the play.

A turtle so slow, but a dancer at heart,
Swirls through the seaweed, it's a fanciful art.
With sardines as sequins, they shimmy and shake,
As laughter erupts with each bellyache.

The sea cucumber slides to the rhythm so sweet,
Providing the bass with its sluggish retreat.
As fish flaunt their colors, they leap with a grin,
All while the barnacles tap dance within.

So let's sing with the tides, join this joyous spree,
With giggles and splashes, in harmony we'll be.
For the waters around us have secrets to share,
In this silly ballet, let's dance without care!

The Language of Flowing Waters

The waves whisper secrets so sweet,
Yet they steal my flip-flops, oh what a feat!
Seagulls caw with glorious flair,
As I dodge their droppings with utmost care.

The tide pulls my towel like it's a game,
Sunburned skin is the only real blame.
I swim like a fish, or so I believe,
But my splash is more like an awkward weave.

A Portrait of the Seaside Tranquility

A sandcastle built with dreams on the sand,
One wave comes and it's all unplanned!
My kids laugh as they splash and they play,
While I search for shade, it's my personal ballet.

The sun is a bully, it won't let me be,
I turn into lobster—come witness the spree!
With sunscreen layers as thick as a pie,
I look more like a mummy, oh my, oh my!

Shadows of the Sunset Waves

As the sun dips low, the colors ignite,
I look like a crab trying to dance in delight.
With my trusty beach chair that just won't recline,
I'm hitting sunset poses, a sight so divine.

The waves stretch their arms, saying "Just take a break!"
I nod, but I fear they'll give me a shake.
My hot dog's gone missing, the gulls are to blame,
Those feathered thieves must be part of the game!

Dancing with Ocean Light

The surfboard balances on dreams so wide,
Yet I tumble and roll, a comedic slide.
Fish are giggling at my awkward stance,
Even dolphins might envy my splashing dance.

With a bucket and spade, I build a grand maze,
But every creation just shouts, "Such a phase!"
The tide laughs out loud, it waves with glee,
I guess it's just Casper, playing with me!

Canvas of the Infinite Blue

In the water, I took a dive,
My floaty pants, oh how they jive!
Fish took selfies with a grin,
While I was trying to fit in.

A crab waved me with a claw so bright,
I waved back, what a silly sight!
Dolphins giggled at my dance,
As I forgot my swimming pants.

A seagull laughed, oh what a tease,
Diving down to steal my cheese.
The waves just rolled with glee and fun,
As seaweed wrapped around my bun.

With each splash, the tide would play,
Making memories in a wacky way.
So here's to the times we dive and swirl,
Where fish wear shades and the seabed twirls.

Whispers of the Coral Reef

Coral colors flash like a quiz,
A fish swam by, looked just like Wiz!
He spun and twirled in the sea so grand,
With gangly fins, oh what a band.

An octopus waved, eight arms in flight,
"Don't bother me, I'm not feeling right!"
With eyes so big and a gooey grin,
I offered him snacks, he let me in.

Sea cucumbers sighed, quite a bore,
"Might you have anything less of a chore?"
I told them jokes, a real big splash,
They wiggled and giggled, made quite a crash.

The clownfish chuckled, swam in loops,
"Might you join our seaweed troops?"
And together we laughed, a silly reprieve,
While bubbles carried our whims to believe.

Beneath the Moonlit Tides

The waves danced under a moonlit glow,
While I slipped, tripped, in water flow!
Caught my breath, what a twist of fate,
Mermaids giggled, deciding my fate.

Starfish told tales of night's delight,
"Don't take that dive, it's quite a fright!"
I laughed and splashed, a ruckus I made,
While jellyfish floated, unafraid.

A whale near mocked with a belly flop,
As I inhaled a mouthful, "Stop!"
"Join the party!" they bellowed in glee,
So I flailed and flopped, oh, what a spree!

With sea turtles guiding my splashy dance,
My fumbles and slips offered humor and chance.
The night we giggled beneath the light,
Swam silly and free, what a glorious sight!

The Siren's Silent Invitation

A siren called with a laugh so clear,
But all I did was trip on my gear!
"Come hither!" she sang, with a wink,
As I hardly managed to not sink.

"Why so clumsy?" a fish did tease,
With bubbles of laughter that flowed like a breeze.
I shrugged and flopped, my pride took flight,
Wishing my floaties were held tight.

The kelp giggled, danced all around,
As I staggered to the seabed ground.
"Swim this way!" called the seaweed band,
As I twirled and spun on my landing sand.

"Here's to the fun beneath these waves,"
Where laughter reigns and the humor saves.
In depths where joy and blunders reside,
Twists of the tide share the laughter wide.

The Soft Gaze of the Sea

A crab wore a hat made of foam,
It wandered far from its sandy home.
With a wink and a pinch, it danced with glee,
Saying, "Why not join my jamboree?"

The waves rolled in with a giggling sound,
Tickling the toes of all on the ground.
They splashed and they dashed, in a playful spree,
Whispering secrets, come splash with me!

Seagulls squawked jokes, oh what a sight,
Clowns of the sky, taking flight in delight.
They'd swoop and they'd dive, then bask in the spree,
Saying, "Life's a beach! Enjoy the sea breeze!"

A fish in a tux danced with flair,
Twisting and twirling without a care.
"Join the conga!" it sang, wild and free,
In this watery world, let laughter decree!

A Chorus of Sea Glass

In a treasure chest where colors collide,
Sea glass giggles, taking pride.
"I'm a gem!" chirps blue, with green in the mix,
While orange blinks, doing a few tricks.

Together they sing, in a bubbly refrain,
"Who needs diamonds? We're fun, not plain!"
The sun hits just right, it's a literal spree,
As they jingle and jangle in joyous jubilee.

A joke is told by a shard of pale green,
"Why did the bottle break? What a scene!
'Cause it couldn't handle our glassy decree,
That life's more fun when you just let it be!'"

Underneath the waves, they throw a big bash,
As dolphins join in with a graceful splash.
"Come dive in," they chant, carefree as can be,
"For life's a treasure, just wait and you'll see!"

Lost in the Currents of Memory

I once found a sock where the gulls like to play,
It danced on the tides, what a wacky ballet!
"The beach needs my style!" it claimed with a plea,
As the waves laughed along, oh what a spree!

A starfish waved back, in its own quirky way,
Saying, "Fashion's important; don't let it sway!"
As a whale plopped down with a marvelous decree,
"Wear what you love, then glide in the sea!"

Seashells chimed in with a musical zing,
Reminding the sock that it's quite the fine thing.
In this whirlpool of memories, all agree,
Funny moments matter more than they seem to be!

As crabs scuttled by, they all took their shot,
Creating a moment that meant quite a lot.
So here's to the laughs, perhaps with some glee,
For life is a journey best lived with esprit!

The Song of the Shimmering Shells

Shells held a concert, a rockin' affair,
With beats from the waves that danced in the air.
A conch blew a tune, oh what a sight!
As clams clapped their edges, feeling just right.

"Oh, pass me the seaweed!" a clam called out loud,
"Because singing's a blast when you're in a cool crowd!"
With a shimmy and shake, they twirled with glee,
As the tide kept the rhythm, setting them free.

A hermit crab strutted, with flair in its step,
"Who needs a house when you've got a cool rep?"
And the sand bubbled up, like joy in the spree,
"Come join in the fun, let your heart truly be!"

With laughter and music under starlit skies,
The shells shared their secrets, wiped tears from their eyes.
And they shouted together, as wild as can be,
"Life's a shell-abration, so come join the spree!"

www.ingramcontent.com/pod-product-compliance
Lightning Source LLC
Chambersburg PA
CBHW072119070526
44585CB00016B/1505